Let's Read About Pets

Budgies

JoAnn Early Macken

Reading consultant: Susan Nations

FRANKLIN WATTS
LONDON • SYDNEY

First UK hardback edition 2004
First UK paperback edition 2005

Franklin Watts
96 Leonard Street
London EC2A 4XD

Franklin Watts Australia
45-51 Huntley Street
Alexandria
NSW 2015

ISBN 0 7496 5758 8 (hardback)
ISBN 0 7496 5825 8 (paperback)

Published in association with Weekly Reader Early Learning Library, Milwaukee.

Printed in Hong Kong, China

Contents

Budgie colours

Budgies can have blue, white, green or yellow feathers. Some budgies have patches or bands of colour.

Feathers

Budgies lose their feathers, or moult, at least once a year. Then new feathers grow.

A budgie's eyes

Budgies can see very well. Their eyes are on each side of their heads. This budgie is looking at you!

Using its beak

A budgie has a curved **beak**. It uses its beak to crack open seeds, clean its feathers and climb.

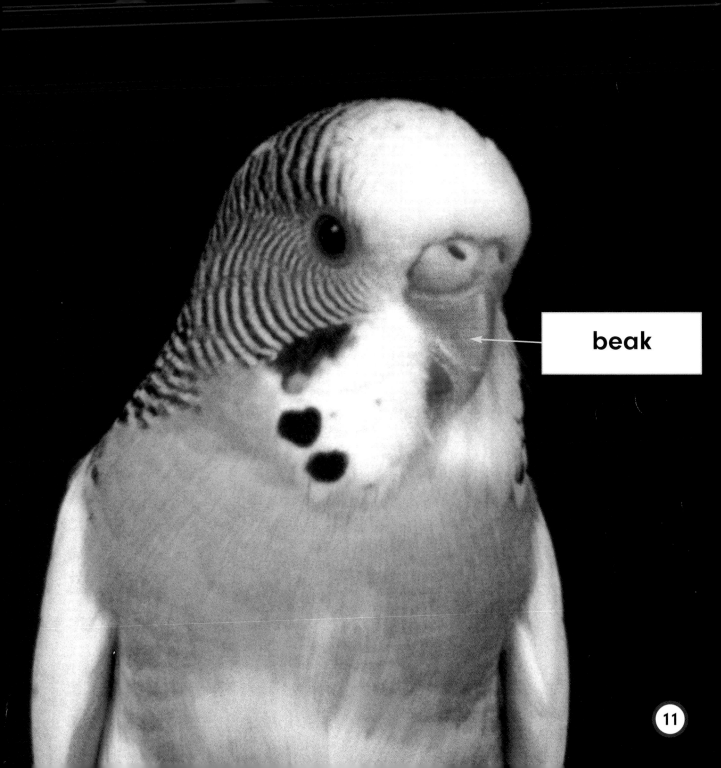

beak

11

Eating and drinking

Budgies need the right food to stay healthy. They eat **seeds**, and fresh fruit and vegetables. They also need fresh water every day.

seeds

Climbing and playing

Budgies climb on perches and ladders. They swing on swings. They like to play with balls and rings.

A happy budgie

Your budgie may perch on your finger. Sometimes it will splash in a birdbath or in a bowl of water.

Flying around

Allow your budgie to fly around for half an hour every day. Make sure all the windows and doors are closed before you open the cage door.

Learning to talk

Budgies can learn to talk like people. Say the same word to your budgie a few times. Your budgie may say it back!

New words

bands — stripes

patches — areas that are different from other areas around them

perch — a place where a bird rests; also to land or rest on something

How to find out more

Here are some useful websites about budgies:

www.pdsa.org.uk/pages/page03_17.cfm
Advice on getting a budgie, its cage, toys, feeding, handling and care

www.dspca.ie/care
Advice on what budgies need

www.petnet.com.au/bird/budgerigar.html
The Budgerigar Page: looking after your budgie and useful advice on keeping a healthy budgie

Note We strongly advise that Internet access is supervised by a responsible adult.

Index

Notes for teachers and parents

This book is specially designed to support the young reader in the reading process. The familiar topic is appealing to young children and invites them to read — and re-read — the book again and again. The full-colour photographs and enhanced text help the child during the reading process. After children develop fluency with the text and content, the book can be read independently.